Wedding Flowers

A wedding design mainly consists of flowers and botanical materials, sometimes of artificial materials.
These provide colour, texture and fragrance, conveying the bride's personality.
At times a structure made of botanical or artificial materials is used as a base.
Various techniques are applied, according to the needs of each individual material and the overall design.
With or without water supply, we need to create a durability that lasts for the wedding day,
always adjusted to each individual material, use and season,
and keeping in mind the quality of the wedding bouquet.

Per, Max and Tomas

Creativity with flowers

Wedding Flowers

Per Benjamin
Max van de Sluis
Tomas De Bruyne

stichting
kunstboek

Wedding wreath to hang around the neck.

The history of wedding flowers

The custom of brightening up wedding ceremonies with flowers dates from ancient times, but the wide selection of wedding bouquets now available has only been a relatively recent development. Until the 19th century we mainly saw wreaths, some crowns and loosely bundled flowers being used for the wedding ceremony. From the early 19th century onwards, wedding flowers and bouquets were more commonly used, ever changing in design and materials, up until today's wide range and almost limitless possibilities.

To show the etymology of wedding flowers and the wedding bouquet itself, the variations in style, uses and techniques, we will take you on a personal journey through history that will bring some understanding and will supply lots of inspiration. Most customs observed today are merely echoes of the past. Flowers, designs and combinations, they all bore a specific and vitally significant meaning. Although most are lost today, they are still incorporated into our modern wedding rituals.

Flowers have followed mankind through the ages, reflecting developments and changes in people's ways of life. A more elaborate use of flowers is first seen in the Mesopotamian and Egyptian kingdoms, where priests and kings ruled. Fantastic palaces and temples were erected in honour of earthly and heavenly powers, all decorated with flowers. Wreaths and garlands were the norm for both men and women, and were used for all celebrations and especially for weddings. Flowers, herbs and foliage were used according to their specific meaning and religious customs, but we know very little about wedding flowers in particular. It is not until we reach Greek times that our knowledge really starts.

In ancient Greece, flowers, wreaths, garlands and small, simple bouquets were sold on town squares. We could say there was a profession of flower binders; one of the first known 'florists' in history was Glycera of Greece. The bouquets were often small and made of wild flowers, violets, olive blossoms and most importantly, roses. Flowers were used to celebrate, praise and communicate, especially when love was involved. To court a girl, for example, a small bouquet was left on her doorstep, while at wedding ceremonies, wreaths were in vogue. Women always used lots of flowers and colours while men mostly used only greenery in theirs, and for the first time in history we see a distinction between male and female use of flowers. Each flower and foliage had its own specific meaning according to the mythology of the gods. Most important were Hera, goddess of matrimony, Aphrodite, goddess of love and her son Hymenaeus, god of matrimony and wedding ceremony.

The symbol of Hera, wife of Zeus and, as a result, also goddess of heaven, is the pomegranate *(Punica granatum)*. For a long time it was, and still is, part of royal regalia and the ceremony of royal weddings.

According to the legend, Aphrodite, goddess of love, was born from the foam of the waves on the sea. When she set foot ashore, water droplets fell from her body and white roses sprung up, symbolizing innocent love. Try to pick these and you get stung by the thorns! The blood, symbolizing passion, colours the roses red and there we have the strongest of love symbols in this world! Some legends even tell that, when rising out of the sea, Aphrodite covered herself with myrtle (Myrthus), which is the symbol of her son, Hymenaeus, god of matrimony. From that time on, myrtle flowers and foliage have been used in wedding wreaths and bouquets.

In ancient Rome, the great metropolis with people from all over the Roman Empire, flowers were an important part of life and were sold all around the city. The influences drew from Greek floral use, continuing and improving on techniques, and an excess of material made possible through better growing techniques and imports from Egypt which led to an opulent and luxurious use of flowers. Romans liked flowers for their colours as well as their scents. They preferred flowers like violets, hyacinths, matthiola, all kinds of herbs and, most importantly, roses. The rose, with its symbolism of love inherited from Greek mythology, now became the flower of fashion. For wedding ceremonies, wreaths worn on the head were fashionable for both women and men, symbolizing fertility and everlasting love, while driving away evil spirits. On very special occasions a crown was made from flowers and foliage. Techniques involved were weaving, sewing and binding, all very delicate flower works often made by the bridesmaids who would gather and make all the flowers for the wedding: wreath, garlands and other decorations, sometimes even small posies meant as a gift to the guests.

In other parts of Europe we see similar traditions. The Celts used herbs, especially garlic, for their bouquets and wreaths, believing they would chase away evil spirits. Flower girls carried sheaves of wheat, a symbol of growth, fertility and renewal. These were replaced with flowers well into Christian times. That changed at the same time as religion brought wedding ceremonies away from people's homes and into the new churches.

But before this, with the fall of the Roman Empire, we enter the Middle Ages. The Christian Church became the new power and the opulent and excessive use of flowers, amongst other things, was banned, being considered a symbol of the old religious mythology and theft from God himself. As a contradiction, and under the pressure of people and traditions, the church itself used many flowers in its symbols. The white Rose symbolised the Virgin Mary, the red Rose stood for Christ. What was spoken 'under the rose' – *sub rosa* – was said in confidence, during confession. The rose, once the most popular flower in Rome, now became a symbol of Christian religion. The wreath, the most common design in the past, was reinvented, symbolizing purity and virginity and was worn by all proven virgin brides for their weddings. Those proven not to be virgins had to marry in shame without a wreath. The wreaths were made out of a mix of flowers, herbs and foliage and were accompanied by a bible in the bride's hands.

The Renaissance brought the rebirth of floral design as it was in old Greek and Roman times, but with a wider use of wreaths. The focus had shifted from a religious towards a secularised, science-driven approach, and this also applied to the use of flowers.

In this period of countless changes the bouquet as we know it today came into being. The Europeans discovered new continents, bringing back, among many things, new flowers. The carrying of a bouquet became fashionable for both royalty and nobility, while the working-class men, if they had any flowers at all, still used the wreath.

In the Baroque and Rococo periods of the late 1600s and 1700s, many new fascinating flowers such as orchids, Chinese roses *(Rosa chinensis)*, peonies *(Paeonia)* and tulips *(Tulipa)* came to Europe, bringing along a wider use of flowers, living ones as well as artificial ones, especially for weddings. The less fortunate tried to copy real flowers out of whatever they had – paper, cloth, pearls … – to decorate and create a wreath or crown for the bride, often combined with colourful dresses with folklore themes.

Cotillion bouquet

The Baroque period, the 'masculine', more pompous and darker of the two periods, rich in materials and colours, was followed by the more 'feminine' Rococo. Graceful and bright, the Rococo trends were once again set by the royal courts, especially the French. Hand-held small bouquets became fashionable, small, round, slightly domed tight bouquets, finished off with a collar of lace or paper and, if really exclusive, in a specially designed bouquet holder of silver or some other valuable material. The most popular flowers were roses, carnations, myrtle and citrus blooms. An even more exquisite bouquet was the one for the *décolletage* of the dress, where often a special glass tube/vase was sewn in for the bouquet.

Another popular bouquet was the *Pompadour* bouquet, named after the times' trend-setter, Madame Pompadour. This light, openly bound bouquet with a collar of paper or lace was provided with a backing, making it easy to lay it down. Other semi-crescent-shaped bouquets were also much in demand.

Pompadour bouquet

During the latter half of the 18th century these bouquets were gradually translated into wedding bouquets and the bouquet slowly started to replace the wreath as the flower design á la mode for a wedding amongst the nobles. The bouquets consisted of short-stemmed flowers loosely put together, randomly mixed, or simply of one variety of flowers with a collar of crêpe-paper or lace. The nobility often combined crown/wreath and bouquet for their weddings. One of the most famous bouquets was the bouquet of Josephine, the first wife of Napoleon, made from violets embedded in lace. Josephine set the trend for the start of the next century with a wider use of wedding flowers/bouquets, but still it was not the norm amongst common people before the mid 19th century that the bride carried a bouquet; more common were the corsage, the wreath, the semi-wreath and the crown.

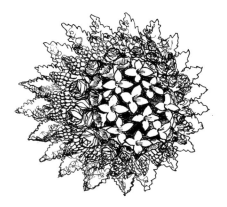

Biedermeier bouquet, cone shaped

Myrtleworks: princess crown, tiara/ semi-wreath and corsage

Wedding wreath for the head, made from artificial materials

It is impossible to compare wedding bouquets from the beginning of the 19th century and the latter part of that century; the differences are enormous, just like most things in society. During the Empire period, most of the bigger cities in Europe had flower markets selling bouquets made up from natural flowers or individually wired flowers, all mixed depending on one's desire; what we would call posies today.

The next big trend in bouquets was the *Biedermeier*; a posy variation with carefully arranged concentric circles of coloured flowers, each ring containing one type of flowers. This tightly-structured bouquet originated from the German-speaking countries in the mid 19th century. First all materials, flowers and greenery are wired, after which circles are created, starting from the centre and tying all along the way, all stems placed parallelly or totally randomly. The spiral system as such did not yet exist. This bouquet, designed during the Biedermeier époque, spread over Europe and was later named after that very same époque.

Biedermeier bouquet, done shaped

Entering the Romantic period in the second half of the 1800s, flowers became more fashionable than ever before, leading to excessive use and variation of designs. The bouquet is now more and more replacing the tradition of holding the bible and the *Hanky-bouquet*, the flower embroidered hanky. It was also the age in which the crown in all various designs and materials was widely spread throughout society, preferably made from myrtle and for the less fortunate creatively made from paper-, cloth-, and pearl-blossoms. In general, bouquets got higher, bigger and more stems were used, this being possible due to a higher quality and better care of the flowers. All over Europe fashionable flower shops appeared, catering for the needs of the rich and successful. Flowers were in fashion! The bouquets took on increasingly advanced shapes and heights, all bent and arranged by means of wires.

In the romantic period, not only the beauty of the flowers was important but much attention was paid to the language of the flowers. The posy had its heyday in Victorian times, when flowers were also the secret messengers of lovers, each flower having its own meaning. Thus bridal flowers were chosen with regard to their traditional significance. In all countries, many books were written on the subject, often conflicting and overlapping each other. Some of the more common flowers and expressions were:
Violets – take me with you
Lily of the valley – I have been adoring you for long
Narcissus – you are too self-complacent
Box – I am faithful forever
Nettle – how can you be so cruel

Unfortunately many lovely flowers were assigned rather undeserved meanings, such as the beautiful anemone (sickness), the delicate purple larkspur (haughtiness) and the sweet-smelling lavender (distrust). As an expression of love, one can easily imagine the complexity of these bouquets!

Whether the end result is formal or loose and unstructured, florists have always employed two methods to create posies: the *natural stems* method (also called hand-tied) and the *fully-wired* method, where the stems of the flowers are removed, replaced by floral wire and constructed into a much lighter posy with an easy to hold handle. There were mainly two different types of binding techniques, the first one starting from the centre and adding more and more flowers on each loop, the second one waiting till the end and tying them all together. The first of the two gives more control and was used for the more elaborate designs. As the name suggests, natural stems posies look more natural and informal, whereas the fully-wired method has a neat, polished effect. The bouquet is becoming an achievable luxury to people of all classes. The white dress is à la mode for the first time in history, replacing the either colourful or black ones for those who could afford it.

The posy got out of favour in the first half of the 20th century, and was followed by the *arm sheaf*, also called the *Bernhardt* bouquet, inspired by the presentation bouquets

Wedding bouquet with tulle collar and myrtus

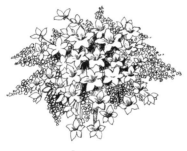
Posy

Shower bouquet with Lovers' knots and small bouquets

given to the actress of the day, Sarah Bernhardt. This design was carried in the arms, a little larger and more dramatic than a posy, with the ribbon or binding treatment being a feature in itself.

The *shower bouquet* replaced the posy as the bridal bouquet of choice around 1910. By 1920 this style became quite exaggerated, with increasingly larger bouquets almost concealing the bride. 'Lovers' knots' were incorporated into the design; yards of ribbons streaming out of the bouquet featured knots along their length into which buds and foliage were inserted. Interestingly, the custom of tossing the bridal bouquet to unmarried girls is only half of the original tradition – the catcher of the bouquet was entitled to untie a lovers' knot and the wish she made was said to come true. Lovers' knots are the evolutionary forerunner of 'swing flowers' – tiny blossoms 'swinging' on narrow ribbons attached to a posy bouquet. The expression à la mode was the nature-inspired bouquet: a bouquet with lots of garden and 'wild' flower materials like peonies, phlox, garden roses, various grasses and foliage with an open cone shape.

After reaching their peak in the 1920s and 1930s, shower bouquets disappeared by World War II; their generously elaborate styles were at odds with the austerely simple suits worn by war-time brides. Corsages, now the sole premise of mothers and grandmothers of the bride and groom, were often worn instead of a hand held bouquet during the war years.

Another fascinating bouquet is the composite-flower bouquet, which dates from the early 20th century. Unable to source the wide range of colours and year-round availability found in today's hybrid roses, florists used this ingenious method of constructing huge 'roses' from the petals of gladioli. Then called 'glameria', these oversized blooms were worn by themselves on a hat or as a corsage or were fashioned into a bouquet for brides with an unlimited budget. At the same time we also see the *Muff*, either made by a dressmaker and then embellished with flowers or made from scratch all out of botanical materials. The perfect choice for the winter wedding! To combine the carrying of the bible and the flowers we also have the *prayer book* or *Bible spray*, where a small bouquet of flowers was attached to the cover of the Bible.

The bouquets remained rather decorative, nature-inspired, with a wide variety of flowers in the same composition or with more classical materials, often using one single flower sort, like rose or carnation with foliage. The technique was wiring and binding, starting with individually wiring each bloom, and creating ranks of four to five blooms wired together. Then, starting at the top, the flowers were bound and bent into position, then added up to four or five ranks and finished off with a little greenery or, according to taste, ribbons and small knots or myrtle wreaths. They were either more open with movement or more strictly static, most of them with an obvious backside with flowers directed forward, and this did not change much until the late 1960s when new styles came in fashion. From the 1970s on we see a rapid change with the introduction of the *formal linear* and *vegetative styles*. Overall we can say that the bouquets

Fully wired rank of roses

Fully wired carnation bouquet

got more attention, and more inspiration and skill was put into them, whereas crowns and wreaths almost disappeared.

Formal linear, the first style to overtake the *decorative* one, was – as the name itself indicates – all about forms of blooms and foliage and lines of stems and branches, where the search for contrasts is crucial. Contrasts in materials, textures and – most significantly – in colours, made this style totally different from the decorative. This gave new challenges to florists in bouquet making and more and more dyed and glittery materials were added into the designs further into the 1980s, all according to fashion in general. Bouquets like the fan enjoyed a fleeting popularity in the late eighties. Lacy plastic fans were embellished with carnations, baby's breath and plenty of tizzy ribbon.

Wedding bouquet from the 70´s
Formal linear style

Cascade or Teardrop bouquet

What used to be termed *the Shower*, now became known as the large, multi-trail bouquet, and was subsequently renamed *the Princess* in honour of the late Princess Diana and her impressive bridal bouquet. The new, smaller shower bouquet regained top position in the 1980s, albeit in smaller sizes. The *Shower* then gave rise to the popularity of the similar *Teardrop*, *Trail* and *Cascade*. These were all variations in proportions, with the most contemporary being the cascade. It featured waterfall-shaped dimensions, the width across the top not much more than the width below. This gave a more natural, flowing look than the stiff point of the teardrop and a neater look than the trail, which peaked in the 1990s.

The *Shower* and single flower expression have been combined in recent years to form a third option called *wrapped stems* – a combination of the two styles where the natural stems are wrapped in beautiful ribbons and pearls.

What we also see in the 1980s and 1990s is an increasing use of twigs, branches and other lines of botanical and artificial kinds, leading us into our next new style, the *transparent style*. This style started in Germany and is best described as a design style in which the use of stems and lines is just as important as the flower heads. These are worked in in an overlapping manner, creating a transparent volume, falling, cascading, rising and moving in one or several directions to become the fashionable design amongst florists. The crescent bouquet personalized this. Perfect for complementing a slim waist and hips, as it has a dainty, curved line.

Nowadays, bouquet designs have become increasingly personal and individual. Styles are often mixed and a variety of accessories is used, focusing on expression rather than on style. Looking back now through history we see how the use of flowers has changed according to historical époques and availability to a constantly larger audience. Like most trends in society, changes took place slowly until the early 20th century. From then on, things started to accelerate and trends have changed constantly from the late 20th century until now, reflecting the tempo of modern life. Styles and shapes, crowns, wreaths, special flowers as well as materials have been reused in various ways and are still incorporated into our wedding rituals today. Today though, in floristry, as in society as a whole, we are looking for a personal expression. There are more things to love than red roses! With knowledge and inspiration from history and with today's fantastic selection and quality of flowers and all other available materials, the options for the designer to convey the message of love and the personality of the bride are limitless!

The future of wedding flowers

Throughout history, flowers have always been used to empower the beauty of the moment. We use flowers in almost every celebration and this certainly applies to our wedding ceremonies, probably the most important occasion of all!
In addition to this, flowers – particularly wedding flowers – are more and more becoming a medium to express ourselves to the world, to friends, family and guests. By means of our wedding flowers, we want to express our individuality, who we are and what we stand for, and how can we do this better then by selecting our own design, flowers, shape, colours, etc.

This of course brings on a new challenge for the florist, demanding good skills and lots of social, human understanding. When translating the emotions, character and will of the bride and groom into our works, we are actually communicating with flowers, colours, textures and materials instead of with words! As a florist we cannot impose our ideas and concepts on the wedding design; we have to listen to what the bride and groom want. We have to shape their dreams to reality. It is becoming increasingly difficult and demanding for a florist to design for a wedding, but at the same time, it boosts the future developments in this field.

Trends in wedding flowers are changing rapidly, reflecting the spirit of the age and the tendencies in society. Some present-day designs, only made to be different and innovative, lack in respect for the flowers. Florists should therefore always comply with the primary rule of respect for the flowers.

Function and beauty have to unite. The first thing that people notice in a bouquet is its colour. Although colour is an important ingredient, it is also one that can change fast, following the fashion. Florists have to lead trends at all times, so don't be afraid to use new combinations. Look at the flowers and detect the differences in their personalities! There are many possibilities, so let the flowers express themselves or use them to reflect a human personality. Use their full potential and combine them with additional materials to enhance your message. Combine artificial and botanical materials. Let your curiosity lead you!

Many wedding designs are too mainstreamed; brides are buying the same glossy wedding magazines and are choosing the same designs. It is our task to stop them here, to show them options, to ask them to put the magazine aside for awhile and to ask them to give you ten minutes to create 'their very own' wedding design. Talk to the bride, ask her about her life and personality, try to understand her as a person and then suggest the wedding design for her! Explain how the suggested shape, colours, flowers and other materials all express and communicate her personality, how they symbolize her!

In future times, the task of the florist will be so much more than only putting together beautiful flowers. It is up to us to match the right flowers, colours, shapes, textures and materials to the feelings, qualities and personality of our clients.
The language of wedding flowers is all about love!

Step by step

Entangled in Love

Designer
Per
Materials
Muscari / grape hyacinth
Olea / olive leaves
Salix / willow
Tillandsia xerographica
Zantedeschia / arum lily
bullion wire
cable ties
floral foam ball
glue gun
newspapers
pearls
pearl headed pins
spool wire

1 It's important to plan your work well. Start by making the wire lines of pearls, pieces of Salix stems and olive leaves. Fix them on paper rolls for easy use later on. Glue the Salix onto the foam ball in a circling movement. Do overlap them and use quite some glue, bearing in mind that this will be the actual 'handle' for the wedding design.

2 Prepare all well watered flowers with 2 to 3 cm of bullion wire and put pearl headed pins on the ends. These are meant for decorative purposes, but also to support the stems when using cable ties to attach them.

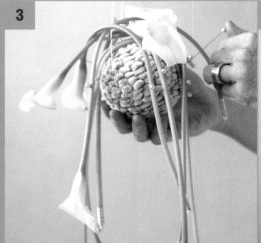

3 The structure on the ball is created with the Zantedeschia, which are attached with long pearl headed pins. Work in both directions and make sure they overlap. To make the flowers as flexible as possible, take them out of the water 12 to 24 hours beforehand, depending on the thickness of the stems.

4 Work in your materials – Zantedeschias, Muscaris, Xerographica and lines of pearls and Salix – in a mixed manner. This creates volume and at the same time the flowers support each other. Be very careful not to damage the fragile Zantedeschia flowers.

Design An arched design expressing movement with entwined stems of flowers in a complex pattern, inspired by the Tillandsia xerographica. Instead of a conventional handle we use an ultra comfortable Salix ball to carry in the palm of the hand, which also perfectly balances the design.
Technique As in many modern designs, a mix of techniques is used here: gluing, pinning, tying, piercing and weaving. Each technique has a functional as well as a decorative purpose.
Emotions The frosted, subdued and clear whites blend into an almost icy but still warm expression; the ideal design for a modern yet traditional winter wedding. I like to express the emotional side of colours and textures in a design.

5 When working in the two trailing ends of the arch, use cable ties to attach the materials. Attach them only to the wired parts of the stem to allow strength and durability.

17

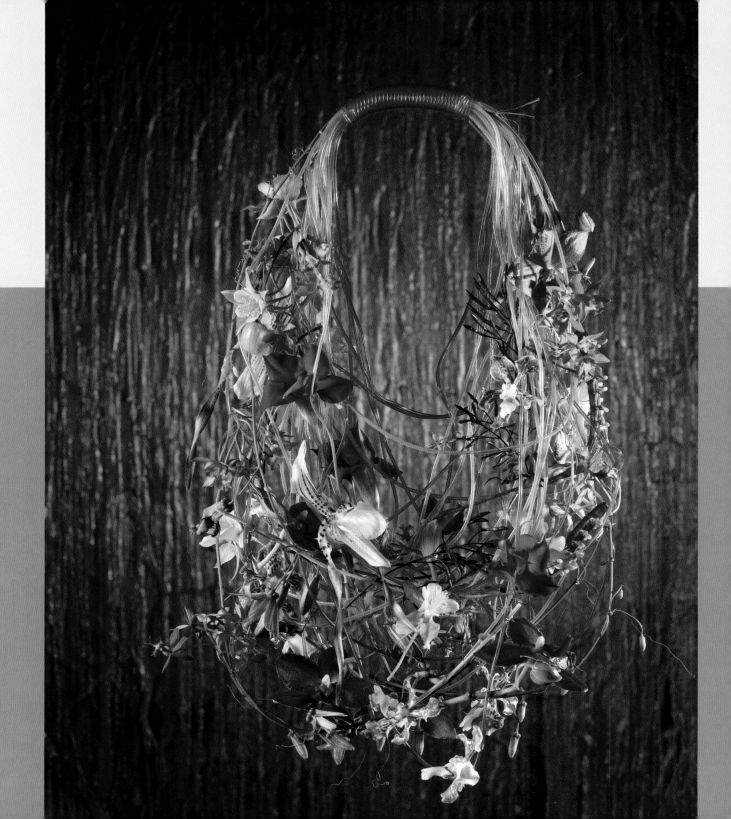

18

Intertwined

Designer
Max
Materials
Aquilegia
Dipladenia
Epidendrum / Epidendrum orchid
Jasminum / jasmine
Paphiopedilum / Slipperorchid
Passiflora / passion flower
Phalaenopsis / moth orchid
Clear Life spray
plastic wire (2 colours)
wax

1 Put together a randomly made up bundle of plastic wires (2 different colours) in your hand and put them together in the desired shape. Make sure that there is enough space left for the flowers. The arrangement should be about 35 to 40 cm long, depending on how tall the bride is. Then tie up the handle with the same wires.

2 Remove the leaves from the tendrils of the Passiflora and the Dipladenia and cut the flowers at a length of about 5 cm. Heat the wax, then dip the ends of the flower stems into the wax to avoid any loss of water. It is very important that the flowers take up as much water as possible. Preferably use warm water for the orchids.

3 Tie the flowers into the wire structure, using the same plastic wire that was used to build the entire construction. It is important to attach the flowers to two lines in order to achieve stability and space in the bouquet. When in doubt you can glue the knots again carefully with cold glue for extra security. Arrange the flowers in an open and airy way, keeping the bulk of the flowers at the bottom and thinning them out as you go towards the handle.

4 In order to stop any additional loss of water, treat the entire bouquet with Clear Life spray once again. Keep a distance of at least 20 cm to avoid frostbite.

Design Refreshing colours and materials. The bouquet holder is also used as the fastening material. The fluorescent characteristic of the plastic wires is repeated in the floral materials and has a strengthening effect.
Technique This design is based on the tying technique: the flowers are tied into the arrangement with the plastic tubes. Make sure that the knot is solid enough. Pay enough attention to the nursing and the preparation of the floral materials; this way the bridal couple will be able to enjoy this arrangement all day long.
Emotions The colour is the focal point of attention: refreshing, uncomplicated and a little daring, possibly a reflection of the bridal couple.

Precious Love

Designer
Tomas

Materials
Rosa 'Tamango' / 'Tamango' rose
Vaccinium macrocarpon / cranberry
cold glue
gold leaf
gutta tape
metal wire
red decorative ribbon
red velvet
rigid cardboard (3 sheets)
spray glue

1 This bouquet is based on a solid collar made from rigid cardboard. The cardboard is coated with soft velvet fabric. Gold leaf and a decorative ribbon are used to create the finishing touch.

2 Cut two squares of 16 x 16 cm from the rigid cardboard and make an opening of 7 x 7 cm in the middle of both squares. Create a handle by attaching a few metal wires to one of the squares. Then put the second square onto the first one so that the metal wires are sitting securely in-between. Tape the two squares together to create a solid base.

3 Put all of the flowers on wire and secure them with tape. The idea is to form a biedermeier so make sure you create a nice spherical shape. Tape the ends together now and again.

4 Scatter little rose buds amongst the biedermeier and secure them with cold glue. Next, distribute the cranberries randomly over the bouquet. Glue a few berries onto the collar of the bouquet; this makes the design look a little looser and more harmonious.

5 Finally decorate a few berries with gold leaf. Start by spraying a few berries with spray glue and attach the gold leaf onto the berries with a small brush. Next, secure the berries on the wedding bouquet with glue.

Design The most classic wedding bouquet will undoubtedly always be the biedermeier. However traditional shapes can be given a contemporary accent by using new materials, flowers, techniques, etc. The square-shaped collar gives this bouquet a modern touch. The use of red velvet radiates passion, but at the same time also tenderness.
Technique Shaping the flowers into a perfect biedermeier is the biggest challenge. It requires an understanding of symmetric proportions; the expansion of the creation in its width, height and depth has to be identical. Fixing the berries on the bouquet is the decorative finishing touch.
Emotions Tender, loving, romantic, precious ... are the key words to describe this wedding bouquet. The design emanates romance spiced with a bit of Christmas atmosphere because of the use of colour, the symmetrical composition and the mastering of the material.

21

Chain of Love

Designer
Per

Materials
Craspedia globosa
Cymbidium / Cymbidium orchid
Gloriosa rothschildiana / glory lily
Hypericum / St. John's worth
Phalaenopsis / moth orchid
Phormium / ornamental grass
Typha latifolia / broadleaf cattail
hard plastic circles
pearl headed pins
spool wire
stapler
thick translucent plastic

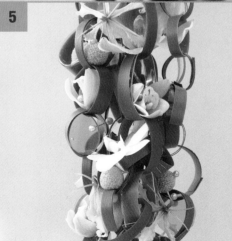

Design A chain of Typha rings, giving us a very flexible and beautifully moving, curving and trailing wedding design. When making the chain longer, you obtain a trailing effect behind the bride. An extreme and modern version of the old teardrop bouquet.

Technique The stapler is used to create a structure consisting of rings. All other materials pinned into this structure. When needed, add some cold glue to secure the materials on the pins. Make the structure the day before and work in the flowers just before the event.

Emotions Love in chains! Strong, powerful and bordering control, but decorative and tender at the same time; concepts fun to play with when secure in your love and relationship. A design that shows off emotions for the self-conscious person who wants to play with the concept of love.

1 Start by making Typha circles/rings in various sizes, some of them lined with the translucent thick plastic, others just made from plastic. Use a stapler that is adjusted to the strength needed for the size of the work you choose.

2 Order the circles according to their size and connect them with each other. Make five to six different lines of 'chains' in various lengths, connecting them with horizontal circles.

3 As a means of carrying the design we make a big thick circle acting as a bracelet. Combine several layers of Typha with a layer of thick plastic. For the inner Typha layer we use glue instead of staples, which might cause small injuries.

4 All flowers and plastic circles are attached with pins inside the individual circles. Put a pin through the flower and put some cold glue on the pin's end. Cover the ends with Hypericum berries for decorative use as well as for safety. Work with well watered materials so you don't need any additional water source.

5 When arranging all materials, think of creating an irregular and flowing rhythm. Group the flowers slightly and arrange them according to their size while descending inside the structure.

23

Flowery Transparency

Designer
Max

Materials
Dipladenia
Epidendrum / Epidendrum orchid
Fuchsia
Gloriosa rothschildiana / glory lily
Paphiopedilum
Passiflora / passion flower
Phalaenopsis / moth orchid
Rosa / rose
Clear Life spray
coloured, transparent PVC
pink spool wire
wax
wire (1,5 mm)

1 Cut two perfectly identical square shapes with circular cut-aways and a diameter of about 20 cm from the PVC. Ensure that both shapes stay connected. Make a mould for the circular shapes so that they are all equal.

2 Carefully wrap four wires of 1,5 mm in pink spool wire. Make a little hook on both ends that can be used to attach the handle to the PVC, once it has been bent into the desired shape. It is important to ensure that the little hooks are properly squeezed tight.

3 Pierce 20 double holes into the PVC using a heated needle. The holes have to be placed in a random order across both surfaces. Cut 20 strands of about 150 cm of the spool wire and feed them through the holes so that both ends join on the inside.

4 Strip the leaves off the Passiflora and the Dipladenia, cut the flowers at a length of about 8 to 10 cm and wax the ends of the stems. In addition you can also apply some Clear Life spray. Tie the flowers to the strands; the easiest way to do this is by suspending the little handbag from somewhere. Start with the tendrils, next work in the largest and most dominant flowers. Create an open arrangement with lots of movement; the flowers should look as if they are 'falling down'.

Design Transparency is the essential ingredient of this bouquet, so make sure that you keep the arrangement very airy. We are aiming to achieve modern romance in which the flowers look like they are covering the bride.
Technique Non-traditional tying technique. In order to ensure that the bouquet can be enjoyed for a long time it is recommended to apply wax and Clear Life spray.
Emotions A romantic bouquet causing you to dream away; the reflection of a carefree bridal couple enjoying pure romance.

Miss Daisy

Designer
Tomas
Materials
Cissus
Rosa 'Piano' / 'Piano' rose
Viburnum opulus / Guelder rose
Xerophyllum tenax / bear grass
green spray paint
plastic tubes + sealing caps
silver-coloured spool wire
strong wire netting
thin silver wire
wire (0,8 mm)

Design The bundled shape of this bouquet fits in perfectly with the country feel of the flowers and tendrils. Using these clusters focuses the attention on the flowers and adds an aspect of tranquillity to the arrangement. The green-red colour combination strengthens the design.

Technique Modelling the chicken wire is the most difficult part of this bouquet. All the flowers have been put in water to ensure a fresh and long-lasting bouquet. This working method also makes the bridal bouquet as light as a feather.

Emotions Intense and carried in a little basket with care. As if you are cherishing all the warm love that is already there and is yet to come. The best and most beautiful things in this world cannot be seen or even heard, but must be felt with the heart. For what the heart gives away is never gone… it is kept in the hearts of others.

1 Select wire netting with small cavities (maximum size of the cavity = diameter of the plastic tubes). The chicken wire should not be too rigid so it remains flexible enough to be bent, yet it should be strong enough to make a solid construction. Small plastic tubes will provide the flowers with water. To make the handle we use 0,8 mm wire.

2 Cut the chicken wire into the desired shape. Draw the shape on paper first on a scale of 1:1. Connect all four sides and the bottom and secure them properly with spool wire, as this is the base of the bouquet.

3 Insert as many plastic tubes into the top part of the bouquet as you can. Spray paint the tubes green beforehand so they do not draw any attention. Fill the tubes with water and put the sealing caps on.

4 Make small clusters of Xerophyllum. Use the same technique for every cluster to ensure a harmonious end result. Put the flowers into the plastic tubes. Distribute them randomly to avoid a stern look. Put in a few tendrils to add a playful touch.

27

Entwined

Designer
Per

Materials
Cymbidium / Cymbidium orchid
Fritillaria / fritillary
Gloriosa rothschildiana / flame lily
Oncidium / Oncidium orchid
Phalaenopsis / moth orchid
Triticum aestivum / common wheat
bullion wire
glass vase
pearl headed pins
soft Mizuhiki wire
spool wire
20-gauge wire

1 Start by preparing your materials; cut the Triticum above the last node and pierce them with 20-gauge wire all the way to the top. Clean the Hypericum and pierce them first with 18-gauge wire and then with soft Mizuhiki wires. Put them aside for later use.

2 Put the Triticum in warm water for one to two hours to make them soft and to prevent them from breaking. Make the actual structure by crossing the Triticum at the middle; twist them around each other two to three times. Start with two and add new ones, continuously crossing and twisting until you reach the desired shape.

3 Instead of an ordinary handle we make two or three rings of Triticum that we attach underneath our structure. Secure the two ends of each ring in the structure itself.

4 Cut the well watered flowers at the right length and prepare them with decorative ends of 2 cm bullion wire and a pearl headed pin. These are then simply attached by weaving them into the Triticum structure.

5 When the first layer is finished, attach a second smaller one on top of the first one and continue adding flowers and Hypericum lengths of soft Mizuhiki wire in the same way.

Design An arched, layered wedding design with an amazing volume and transparency, elegantly carried on top of your hand with a ring fitting! My intention is to show the delicacy of each and every flower in this design.
Technique The first technique is that of the 'hand made chicken wire'; work precisely, try to visualize the final shape and work towards that. For the flowers we use the weaving technique, after which everything is secured by tying the lines of Mizuhiki into the structure.
Emotions A back-to-nature feeling; honest values and colours from fields of grass blowing in the wind. A design for the modern, natural and environmentally conscious bride who wants to express herself.

29

Pure White

Designer
Max
Materials
Convallaria majalis / lily of the valley
Eucharis grandiflora / Amazon lily
Eustoma russellianum 'Echo Pure White'
Hedera / ivy (leaves)
Stephanotis floribunda / Madagascar jasmine
cotton wool
rubber band
silver wire (0,28 mm)
small pins
white ribbon
wire

1 Create a little hook at the end of the silver wire and secure it in the top part of the Convallaria. Insert the wire smoothly amongst the little flowers, attach some cotton wool to the end of the stems, elongate these and wrap the cotton wool tightly around the stem.

2 Take the 0,8 mm wire and create a little hook at the end. Roll this up together with cotton wool into a small fluffy ball. Cut the wire at the bottom in a sharp-pointed end and pierce the wire carefully through the Eucharis. Wrap the bottom of the stem in cotton wool and put them in a vase with water together with the other flowers.

3 Wrap the Stephanotis and the Eustoma in cotton wool and lengthen the stems with wire. Tape up all the flowers with rubber or floral tape.

4 Now we can start to assemble the bouquet. Start from the middle and work your way around as you go downwards. Do not put in all of the flowers at the same height but create some depth. Tie the wire together now and again with a thin rope; when doing this make sure that the connecting point does not move downwards. Finish the bouquet using the Hedera leaves which have also been put on wire. Wrap the white ribbon carefully around the handle and secure it with little pins.

Design A classic arrangement with a modern touch: although the shape and choice of flowers are traditional, the bouquet looks contemporary because the foliage has been left out.
Technique The technique used is traditional and very practicable. It is very important to pay attention to the right treatment of the individual types of flowers, as it makes them more solid and will increase the durability of the bouquet.
Emotions This design reflects pure emotions because of its colour and the clear choice of flowers, it is traditional yet contemporary, the perfect fit for a lot of brides today.

31

Soft Circles of Eternal Love

Designer
Tomas
Materials
Phalaenopsis / moth orchid
Tillandsia xerographica
cold glue
hot glue gun
icicle (as a handle)
white spool wire
wire (0,8 mm)

1 This is a wintry bouquet in shades of white and grey, decorated with powdery snow. The 0,8 mm thick wire forms the base; the elegant handle is made from a cylinder dusted in snow spray.

2 Make two circles of different sizes (4 and 8 cm diameter). Attach five bent wires to these. Then model about 23 circles of different sizes. Put the circles in a random shape and connect them, using white spool wire.

3 Attach this base of circles to the handle. Apply several layers of spray paint to paint everything white. Make sure you spray from a distance to avoid dripping. Spray some glue onto the base and scatter some powdery snow on top of the construction; this makes the wintry effect complete.

4 Secure the Tillandsia with cold glue on the inside of the circles. Do this in different places; it ensures that the bouquet keeps its transparency and elegance.

5 Next, attach the flowers with cold glue. Put the large flowers at the top and the smaller ones at the bottom. Also use more flowers at the top than at the bottom. Add some more powdery snow as a finishing touch.

Design A carefully constructed, transparent waterfall of circles is the base for this bridal bouquet. The refined lines of the Tillandsia break the tight geometrical shapes and add the necessary elegance. The shades of white and grey and the powdery snow give a wintry accent to this bouquet. As there is a big concentration of flowers at the top, the bouquet looks lighter at the bottom.
Technique Several circles are modelled and then connected to form a certain shape. The circles are decorated on the inside with Tillandsia. Securing the flowers with glue adds the finishing touch to this bouquet.
Emotions Marriage is like a never-ending circle, an eternally rippling stream of inexhaustible energy. Living together in an eternal circle is only possible if you love each other unconditionally.

33

Circle of Love

Designer
Per
Materials
Cambria / Cambria orchid
Dendrobium / Dendobrium orchid
Hypericum / St. John's worth
Malus (fruit) / apple
Muscari / grape hyacinth
Xerophyllum asphodeloides / eastern turkeybeard
bullion wire
cable ties
Mizuhiki wire
pearl headed pins

Design Design with many aqua colours spanning from green to blue, showing the unlimited possibilities of colour in a wedding design. The main theme in this design is the way it is carried in your palm and the resulting movement in it!

Technique The apple is used as a basis into which all other materials are pierced. The flowers are then attached to this structure with pinning and weaving techniques, using cable ties, pins and bear grass. Always bear in mind that botanical materials shrink when drying, therefore secure everything well!

Emotions Relaxed, joyful, almost childish and definitely different! There is a wedding design for each and every woman, each and every personality. Not all designs should be white, romantic and decorative. On the contrary!

1 Make circles with the Mizuhiki wires, using different lengths to create 'loops' of various sizes. Stick them to the apple on a horizontal level 1/3 up from the bottom. Entwine the wires to create stability, weaving each new wire into the other ones.

2 Work in the bear grass in the same way as the Mizuhiki wires, sticking the thicker end into the apple and securing the thinner end with a cable tie. Also add some wires with Hypericum berries pierced onto them.

3 Attach 2 cm of bullion wire to the Muscaris and put a pearl headed pin at the end for decorative purposes as well as to give them the strength needed for attaching them. Weave in the Muscaris and use cable ties to secure them.

4 Work in the Muscaris in a flowing, crossing manner, 2/3 clockwise and 1/3 anticlockwise to create movement. Take some longer Muscaris and let them trail.

35

Circle of Love

5 Pre-pierce both the Hypericums and the Dendrobium orchids on the bear grasses. Use well watered materials and do this as closely as possible to the wedding ceremony.

6 Add an orchid to most of the trailing bear grasses, secure them with cold glue and end with a Hypericum. This adds beautiful movement to the design when carried.

7 Finally add some Cambria orchids. They function as focus flowers and also connect all colours beautifully. Use pearl headed pins in matching colours.

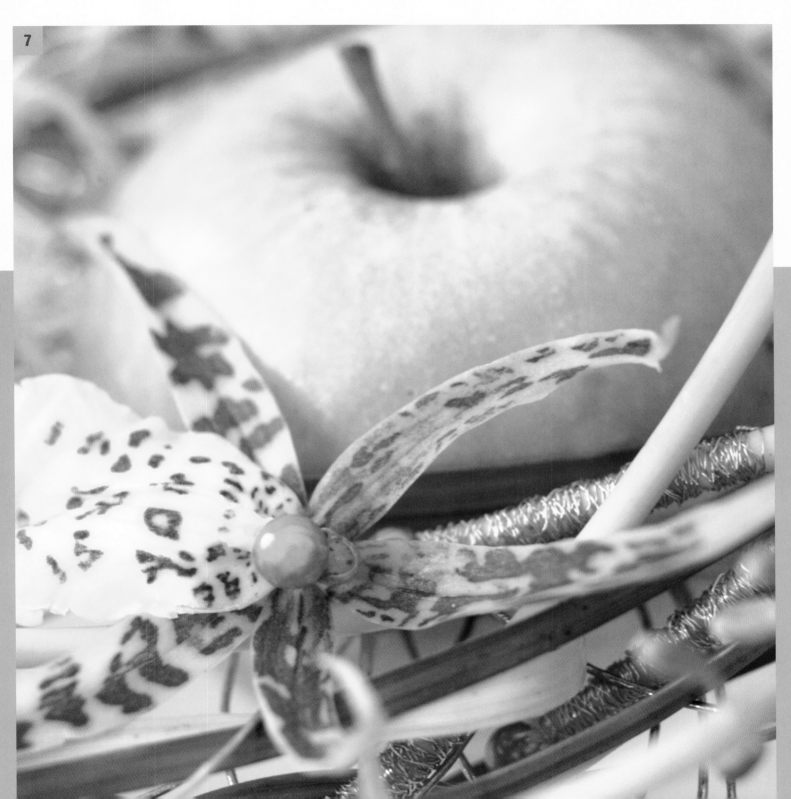

Interwoven Connection

Ontwerper
Max
Materialen
Aspidistra / cast iron plant
Fritillaria assyriaca / fritillary
Orchids
black spool wire
Clear Life spray
cold glue
leaf shine

Design This bridal bouquet in the shape of a handbag has been constructed from a structure of Aspidistra leaves that have been woven together. The interwoven leaves are the symbol of marriage. The lines trailing down give the arrangement an elegant and frivolous appearance.

Technique This bouquet uses different techniques which have been combined; in the case of the Aspidistra leaves for example the threading technique is combined with the interweaving of the strands. The flowers are secured with the gluing technique. Make sure everything is processed in a really solid way to ensure that the bride can enjoy it all day long.

Emotions Interwoven leaves – interwoven lives. Flowers originate from the middle just like beautiful things shall originate from this alliance.

1 Take the Aspidistra leaves and tear off small strips of about 1 cm wide lengthwise (follow the direction of the veins). Clean the strips by wiping them with a soft moist cloth that has been sprayed with leaf shine. Do not spray the leaf shine directly onto the leaf, as this creates an artificial appearance.

2 Cut the black wire at a length of about 150 cm. Thread the wire through the pieces of Aspidistra, using loops of about 8 cm. Finish at the end of the leaf. Move the leaves a little bit closer together, making them rounded. Next interweave the strands of leaves, starting from a circle of about 25 cm. Go through the openings between leaf and wire which will help you to achieve a beautiful structure, the bottom part being fatter and fuller and the rest of the arrangement thinning out as you go towards the top.

3 Treat the leaves with Clear Life spray. Make sure you keep the spray at a sufficient distance when applying it. Check the stability of the bouquet, the arrangement should be solid and compact. Secure the flowers with glue in-between the Aspidistra leaves (ensure that the stems have been properly waxed). Set out the main lines first and work your way simultaneously from two sides to keep the balance in the bouquet. Strip the leaves off the Fritillaria to make the beautiful stem stand out.

Connected

Designer
Tomas

Materials
Fritillaria persica / fritillary
Hydrangea
Lilium longiflorum / Easter lily
Stephanotis floribunda / Madagascar jasmine (tendrils)
Tulipa / tulip
decorative beads
decorative pins
hot glue gun
packaging tape
raffia (natural)
rigid cardboard
wire (0,8 mm)
wool

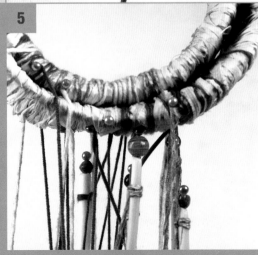

1 Rigid cardboard and strong wire (0,8 mm) are the basis of this bouquet. Do not use any corrugated cardboard, as this will crack or break far too quickly. Packaging tape will help join everything together.

2 Create perfect circles of approx. 13 and 16 cm by modelling several wires around a circular-shaped object. Put these on the inside of the cardboard circles. Secure everything with tape. Wrap the circles in raffia. Apply the glue on the outside of the smallest circle, and on the inside of the largest circle to ensure no glue residues are visible.

3 Wrap some wool around the two circles in certain areas to create a beautiful flow and movement when the two circles are combined.

4 Use decorative pins to attach woolen strands to the circles. Make sure you insert the pins at an angle so they do not pierce the circles completely. The rigid cardboard is an excellent hard basis to pierce into.

Design The design is determined by two circles which are interwoven and hence form one entity. The flowers are cascading down like a waterfall, creating a graceful, transparent entity. This is the perfect bouquet for brides who like a modern and smart appearance.
Technique The most difficult aspect of this design is creating two perfect circles which fit into one another. Be sure to use durable and strong cardboard and wire with a minimum thickness of 0,8 mm. Decorative pins are used to secure the woolen strands which are used to attach the flowers to.
Emotions Two rings as a sign of unity, the ultimate symbol of marriage. Nothing is more important than sharing each other's individuality while forming a united connection.

5 Next, work your flowers into the design. Decorate the ends of the flowers with small stones and beads to add an additional decorative touch. Use the Stephanotis tendril to create a harmonius green line. Finally secure some Hydrangea here and there with glue, acting as little highlights in the creation.

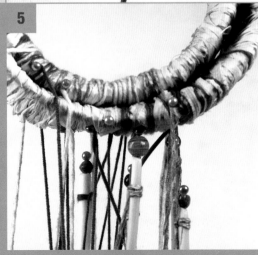

41

Fragile and Tender as Love

Designer
Per

Materials
Convallaria majalis / Lily of the Valley
Salix / willow
bullion wire
chiffon ribbons
glass cylinder vase
pearl headed pins
pearls
ribbon wire
silver foil tape
spool wire

1 Spin the spool wire around several cylinder shaped vases of different sizes. Clean some beautiful big Salix stems and put the Convallaria in some water. Use the cultivated sturdy ones instead of the more fragile wild specimen for durability.

2 Take all wire bundles and put them together, adding some lines on which you have pierced Salix flowers. Tie together the part where all wires connect to form the handle. Use spool wire and cover it with a layer of ribbons for a comfortable feel.

3 Prepare the Convallaria with 2 to 3 cm of bullion wire and a pearl headed pin, making the wired part sturdy enough to attach to the wire structure. Make lines with pearls and Salix for decoration later on.

4 Let the wire structure hang free to show transparency. Attach the Convallaria and put the flowers in both directions. Create the biggest volume in the thicker lower part, elegantly thinning out towards the handle.

5 Use the silver foil tape to secure the Convallaria. It is technically good and decorative at the same time. Make sure you dry all stems beforehand, the silver foil does not work well on wet surfaces!

Design A design which is technically and aesthetically adjusted to one flower, the Convallaria. A fragile, delicate, elegant and quite short-lived flower, showing all aspects of its character.
Technique Wired nest in the shape of a handbag in which the Convallarias are fixed with silver foil tape. Bear in mind that the tape works best on dry surfaces. Weave the flower heads into the wires and let the bells rest on them. This will keep them good-looking even when fading slightly!
Emotions Chic, elegant, transparent and delicate! A handbag design with the chicest of women in mind. Imagine Jackie Kennedy in a short dress, gloves and hat! Something for the less formal wedding!

43

Natural Romance

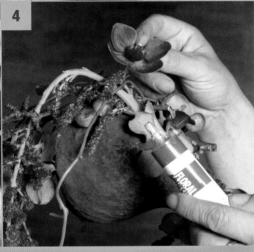

Designer
Max
Materials
Amaranthus caudatus / love-lies-bleeding
Aristolochia / Dutchman's pipes
Lonicera sp. / honeysuckle
Malus
Nerine bowdenii / Guernsey lily
Phalaenopsis / moth orchid
Vanda / Vanda orchid
Wisteria sinensis / wisteria (fruits)
cold glue
dried seed pod
wax

1 Carefully remove the leaves from the tendrils of the Lonicera, the Wisteria, the Malus twigs and the Aristolochia. Make sure that the tendrils do not break or get damaged. We will need them to set out the lines later on.

2 Heat up the white wax in a saucepan. The wax should be fluid, but should not be overheated. Cut off the flowers from the Phalaenopsis and Vanda twigs and dip the ends into the wax. Do the same thing with the other materials at the time when you cut them at the desired length.

3 Clasp the Malus twigs in the dried seed pod, making sure that they are arranged in a spatially attractive way and trailing down on both sides. Secure the twigs with a little drop of cold glue.

4 Secure the other materials into the pod with glue, starting with a few Aristolochia twigs to put some emphasis on the movement. Then work in the heavier materials first. Make sure that you retain lightness and movement in the bouquet.

Design An open dried seed pod is used as a base, which is also used as a handle to hold the bouquet. Natural materials are used to create a bouquet which is cascading down from this central point. A few beautiful orchids give the arrangement a glorious finishing touch.
Technique It is very important to prepare the materials properly so that they will last all day long. Allow the cold glue to dry for about 10 seconds before use. Be aware of the fact that excessive use of glue does not make your arrangement any more solid or more beautiful.
Emotions This arrangement has a cheeky, relaxed appearance yet it is very natural. The bouquet can be carried in a comfortable way. With every single step movement is created in the bouquet, giving the bouquet as well as the bride a very elegant appearance.

45

Sheer Sensuality

Designer
Tomas
Materials
Anthurium crystallinum / flamingo flower
Celosia / cockscomb
Phalaenopsis / moth orchid
Stephanotis floribunda/ madagascar jasmine
cold glue
decorative pins
rigid cardboard
tape
wire (0,8 mm)

1 A piece of rigid cardboard, tape and wire (0,8 mm diameter) are the basic elements used for this bouquet. The botanical part is made up by the strong Anthurium leaf and the Phalaenopsis.

2 Draw three veil shapes (scale 1:1) on a piece of rigid cardboard and cut them out. Do not use any corrugated cardboard to avoid cracks. To ensure the stability attach strong wire to the cardboard and secure it with tape. Then bend everything into the desired shape.

3 Stick the leaves onto the cardboard using double-sided tape. Allow the leaves to dry a few hours before using them to make sure they are quite flexible to process and will not crack or rip too quickly.

4 Put the flowers only on the front and top of the base. Leave a space between every flower and the base in order to achieve a floating effect. Insert the pin into the nose of the flower and glue the little stem of the flower and the top of the pin together so that everything is properly attached. Put in a tendril of Stephanotis to break the stern line of the composition.

Design This is an uncommon design, in which the botanic material is draped over the wrist and the flowers are 'floating' on top of the base. The dark structure of the leaf combined with the pristine white flowers adds extra value to the bouquet.
Technique First of all the three basic structures are drawn and modelled. It demands a bit of precision work to attach the leaves afterwards onto this base with double-sided tape. The delicate orchids are pinned onto the base, but are nevertheless well protected because the base is so solid.
Emotions The flowers move just like butterflies and they flutter about on top of the bridal bouquet. It radiates a nice feeling, like having butterflies in your stomach for the big day.

Passionate

Designer
Per
Materials
Gloriosa rothschildiana / glory lily
Guzmania
Hypericum / St. John's worth
Nerine bowdenii / Guernsey lily
Phalaenopsis / moth orchid
bullion wire
cable ties
hole maker tool
paper rolls
pearls
pearl headed pins
plastic strings
spool wire
translucent plastic

Design A bracelet as a wedding bouquet! Very comfortable to carry and beautiful in a more relaxed and elegant way than holding something in the hand. The focus is on the character of the materials. Strong expressive materials such as the plastics match with the Gloriosa in a vibrant design.

Technique Wiring, weaving and tying, according to the need of the design or of each single material. Please test the durability of the materials before using them in a final product. Also bear in mind that they behave differently depending on the season.

Emotions Hot colours, hot temper? Not necessarily. It can also be translated as energy, dynamics, creativity and lots of will! A wedding design for the more daring and outspoken bride or simply matching a wedding dress in any other colour than white.

1 The translucent plastics are crucial in this design. The thick and sturdy plastic is used for the base (the bracelet), the thinner one for the decorative effects, while the stretchy plastic is used in the trailing part.

2 Make a bracelet from the thick plastic, overlapping some 10 cm. Use a belt hole maker to make holes and tie the bracelet together with plastic strings. Use long lengths, tie them together irregularly to create volume and build some kind of structure for the flowers.

3 Prepare lengths of wired material, pearls, squares of plastic, Hypericum berries, Guzmania leaves and Nerines. Good order makes further work lots easier!

4 Hang the bracelet freely to allow easy access to work. Place lines in an irregular pattern and overlapping flowing manner to add body and volume, always securing all materials.

51

5 Add the more dominant flower heads, such as Gloriosa and Phalaenopsis in proportion to size and placement. Finish off with wire lines of Nerine and secure with some final wire lines of pearls.

6 Prepare the Gloriosa by making a decorative end with bullion wire and pearl headed pins. Weave them in between all lines of plastic and wire. Be very careful when creating volume for the fragile materials.

Bracelet

Designer
Max

Materials
Ceropegia woodii woodii / string of hearts
Dendrobium / Dendrobium orchid
Dendrochilum / Dendrochilum orchid
Orchid tendrils
Phalaenopsis / moth orchid
Rosa / rose
bullion wire
coarse needle
transparent PVC
white beads

Design A bouquet which is made to be hand-held but which can also be worn as a bracelet. The thin, long strands of the arrangement move in tandem with the bride and create an elegant effect, which is strengthened even more by the transparency in the bouquet.
Technique Everything starts with a good base: because of its transparency everything is clearly visible in this bouquet, so make sure everything is neatly tied and cut. If you follow the step-by-step plan meticulously, you should not have any difficulties creating the different layers of this bouquet.
Emotions This bouquet is very contemporary with regards to the processing technique, the proportions and the way in which it is carried. It exudes a noble romantic feeling but due to its length, agility and transparency it is also very elegant.

1 Cut a strip of about 8 cm wide from the PVC which can be slipped over the hand. Pierce holes in both ends using a coarse needle and sew these together with bullion wire or alternatively with nylon wire. Make two holes right next to each other with the same needle and repeat this several times, dividing the holes at random across the entire surface area of the bracelet. Put the wires through these holes and allow them to stick out, as they will be used later on to fasten all the materials to.

2 Make strands with the Dendrobium and the roses, divide them at random over the wire and make them look natural by fastening the flowers to the side. This way we will achieve the same effect as a leaf growing on a twig.

3 Drape the flower strands on top of the PVC and secure them with the wires which are sticking out. Do the same thing with the Ceropegia, the wires with the beads and the orchid tendrils. Mix up the different materials when processing them to create some depth and to give the impression that they have become entwined naturally.

4 Then work in the other flowers such as the Phalaenopsis and secure them with glue. Be aware not to glue the flowers on top of the PVC and the wire structure as one solid layer, but create a multitude of layers which will result in a nice line pattern. The bouquet has to look good from all sides; make sure you regularly look at the arrangement from different angles while you are working on it.

Exotic Fan

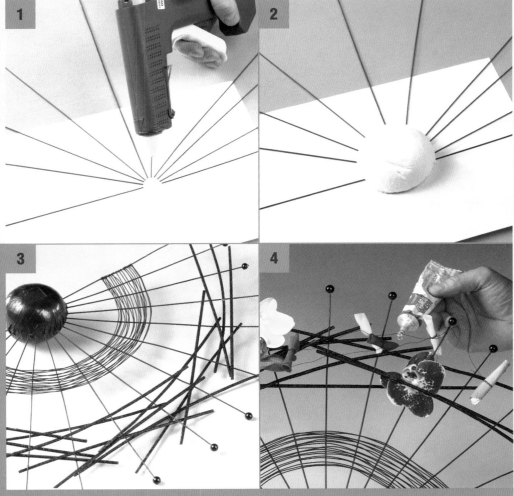

Designer
Tomas

Materials
Dendrobium / Dendrobium orchid
Oncidium / Onchidium orchid
Phalaenopsis / moth orchid
Rosa 'Cool Water' / 'Cool Water' rose
Rosa 'Passion' / 'Passion' rose
Rosa 'Sonrisa' / 'Sonrisa' rose
black elastic tape
black pearls
black spray paint
cold glue
decorative spool wire
hot glue
metal wire
sparkling decorative sticks
Styrofoam ball (9 cm diameter)
thin black decorative wire
wire (0,7 mm)

1 Arrange the wires in the shape of a fan. Put them on a piece of paper so you can easily secure them with hot glue without damaging the base. Make sure to distribute the little bars evenly.

2 Cut the Styrofoam ball into two equal parts and secure these with hot glue onto the ends of the wires as if all the lines are starting from this central point. Repeat this also on the other side so we end up with a ball which will serve as a handle. Next cover the ball completely and tightly with black elastic tape.

3 Weave the metal wire through the radial course of lines. About 20 times should be enough to create a solid base. Spray paint the construction black. Then put some decorative sticks at the top to give the bouquet a wider dimension which will serve as a base for the flowers. Decorate the wires by fixing a black pearl to each of them with glue.

4 Roll up the flower petals using decorative spool wire and create a garland. Use cold glue to secure all the flowers to the wooden sticks. Insert them at different depths in order to put some more life into the bouquet. Distribute the colours and sizes of the flowers evenly over the bouquet.

Design A wedding bouquet with a remarkable and unusual shape. This fan-shaped bouquet with orchids gives us an exotic feeling. The bright colours that come with it complete the picture.
Technique The construction and the botanical materials used are the most important elements in this design. By interweaving solid metal wire and spool wire, it is possible to achieve the desired construction. The focal point of the design is a decorative ball which also serves as a handle.
Emotions Allow your happiness to flourish and fan out. All the intense and pure moments spring from the core of your being. It is only when you share these moments with the people around you, that they become valuable.

Modern Romance

Designer
Per
Materials
Eucalyptus
Hypericum / St. John's worth
Limonium 'Emille' / sea lavender
Rosa 'Cool Water' / 'Cool Water' rose
Viburnum (fruit)
chiffon ribbons
floral tape
metal angle hair
pearl headed pins
spool wire
wool
20-gauge wire

1 This design is all about colour and texture. It all started with the multicoloured wool I found, from which I built out colour and texture in both accessories and flowers. Important here is the graduation in small steps, creating a fine toned spectrum of browns and pinks.

2 Create a perfect dome ending in an exact 90 degree angle, all very classic and beautiful. Start by wiring and taping the well watered flowers. To avoid problems, do pre-measure them all according to the desired size of your bouquet. Group them irregularly according to texture and colour with clear dominances.

3 Finish the underside with Limonium 'Emille' all the way into the binding point. Cut off the wires gradually, creating a thinning long pointed handle. Secure this with floral tape and cover with angle hair and finally a layer of bullion wire. The pearl headed pins are meant as ornament and to secure the binding place.

4 Now it's time to decorate! Use pre-made lines of Hypericum and Eucalyptus leaves on spool wire, wool and several ribbons, all attached and secured with pearl headed pins. Create flow and movement and be aware not to cover more than 1/3 of the surface.

Design The classical decorative wired wedding bouquet in a new colour spectrum with the focus on the decorative elements. A modern approach of the flower-rich decorative style for the woman of today.
Technique Wiring and taping techniques. Be aware to use well watered materials if you do not use any water supply. Do not attach any of the decorative elements to the roses to avoid damage to the flowers.
Emotions Romance – a classical shape with modern colours! Colour is the strongest way to communicate emotions and personality, so make use of that! A design for the modern, decisive, daring and romantic woman!

Composite Unity

Designer
Max

Materials
Elaeagnus / Russian olive
Epidendrum / Epidendrum orchid
Rosa / rose
cold glue
needle
nylon wire
round wood chisel
wire (0,6 mm)

1 Take fifteen large-flowered roses, remove the petals and sort them according to size (preferably four different sizes). Cut the 0,6 mm wire into little pieces of about 2 cm and bend these into clips. When cutting the ends of the clips ensure they are sharp-pointed.

2 Select the most beautiful rose and remove the outer leaves. Make the rose a little bit more compact by piercing some clips into it. Apply a very thin layer of cold glue onto the inside of the bottom 30% of ten of the smallest petals. Allow the glue to dry for about ten seconds before pressing the petals against the rose. Make sure you follow the normal rhythm of the rose so that it stays looking natural. To give the arrangement additional stability, put in some more clips after every two circles that you complete around the rose.

3 Arrange the Elaeagnus leaves in little stacks of ten. Use a wood chisel to knock little circles out of the Elaeagnus and store them in little stacks.

4 Thread the Elaeagnus circles (the silver side up) onto the nylon wire using a coarse needle. Leave some random spaces here and there between the Elaeagnus circles. Create seven different strands using this method.

Design Using a few botanical materials we create new ones, based on the original material. The rose gains strength and the circles made from the Elaeagnus leaves provide the surprise effect. The bouquet is carried on the hand and the strands of Elaeagnus follow every move with elegance.

Technique The method used to make the composite rose is more compact than the traditional one. Partly due to the glue a large area of the surface is sealed and is unable to let any water through. This way the rose can be kept fresh much longer, which makes it exceptionally suitable for wedding bouquets.

Emotions The design is romantic because of the oversized rose, but also elegant because of the moving Elaeagnus lines. This is a bouquet which makes the bride look graceful and agile.

5 Secure the strands onto the composite rose with longer clips and cold glue. Pay attention to the three-dimensional aspect when working in all the floral materials and make sure that there is enough room left to hold the bouquet comfortably. Work in the Epidendrum and let it trail down from the rose.

61

My Love ...

Designer
Tomas

Materials
Gypsophila paniculata / baby's breath
Rosa 'Te Amo' / 'Te Amo' rose
Symphoricarpus albus / snowberry
cold glue
floral tape
1 large red pearl
red pearls
red spool wire
red spray paint
wire (0,8 mm)

Design The large red expanding rose is pure romance. A classic design, approached from a modern point of view. The white snowberries and the Gypsophila make a nice change and give the bouquet a nice and fresh finishing touch.
Technique New in this design is the base construction of woven wires onto which expanding rose petals are glued into a composite rose. Be sure to select appropriate roses if you want to dry the bouquet later on.
Emotions The symbolism of flowers and colours is very strongly present in this arrangement. The rose is the symbol of love; the Gypsophila is the symbol of fertility. The red rose says: 'I love you!' and whispers with a white touch: 'Trust me.' When both colours are used together in the bridal bouquet, the message is: 'I want to be with you forever.'

1 Put a straight wire in the middle and attach seven bent wires to this starting point. Tape everything together using floral tape. Spray paint everything red. Next connect the wires, starting from the centre. The little bar in the middle is the core onto which the rose will be attached later on.

2 First of all the handle is to be finished. Wrap the taped-up wires of the handle in red decorative spool wire. Decorate the end with a large red pearl.

3 Cover the top end of the middle wire with cold glue. Put a rose on top which has been cut off just underneath the crown petals.

4 Secure the rose petals with cold glue on the rose in the middle and on the construction. Enlarge the open spaces between the petals as you work towards the outside. Glue the petals around the core in-between the wires in several places in order to achieve a solid base. Finally, use the Gypsophila and the white snowberries which are secured with glue in one flowing movement.

Summer Fan

Ontwerper
Max
Materialen
Aquilegia / columbine
Jasminum polyanthum
Lathyrus odorata / sweet pea
Passiflora 'Victoria' / 'Victoria' passion flower
Phoenix washingtonia / washingtonia palm tree
Rosa / rose
bullion wire
cold glue
waterproof tape
wax

1 Take two Phoenix leaves which have not been torn and cut them into a round shape, making sure that they are both 100% alike.

2 Wrap the stems of the Phoenix along a length of about 7 cm in two different colours of bullion wire. Make sure to work with the utmost precision to achieve a neat and tidy end result. Then connect the two leaves, using waterproof tape. Carefully unwind a piece of tape of about 5 cm long, together with bullion wire.

3 Cut the flowers at a length of about 10 cm. Make sure they have taken up plenty of water before you cut them. Dip the end of the stems into liquid wax to avoid any loss of water. Remove most of the leaves from the Passiflora but keep the nodes.

4 Secure the flowers with glue amongst the Phoenix leaves. Start with the roses (these are the most compact and the strongest) and attach the Passiflora on top afterwards with an airy movement. Then work in the other flowers. Make sure you create enough depth between the flowers so that the arrangement looks playful, rich and abundant.

Design In this arrangement it is very important that the two leaves are identical; the same goes for the colours of the bullion wire and the flowers. When dividing the flowers adopt an airy and not too mathematical approach in order to create a romantic and a wealthy nonchalant feeling.
Technique The base of leaves is wrapped in wire; the flowers are secured with glue. Make sure you work very precisely and neatly so that no glue residues are visible.
Emotions A frivolous and playful decorative summery fan bouquet, which says a lot about the bridal couple and their approach to life.

65

Together is Stronger

Designer
Per

Materials
Fritillaria meleagris / fritillary
Galanthus nivalis / snowdrop
Hypericum / St. John's worth
Tulipa / tulip
cold glue
floral tape
glass pearls
pearl headed pins
spool wire
Styrofoam ball
20-gauge wire

1 When creating this Tulipmelia – a flower made of tulip petals – it is extremely important to use fresh and well watered tulips, guaranteeing a long-lasting design. The same applies to the Galanthus.

2 The base is made from a Styrofoam ball. First make a ring fitting from 20-gauge wire, fix it with floral tape and cover it decoratively with gold spool wire. Push the ring fitting into the Styrofoam ball and secure it. Do not forget to measure the size of the ring so that it fits the bride!

3 When making the Tulipmelia use cold glue to avoid damage to the very fragile and thin petals. Work your way outwards and downwards until you reach the ring itself and have covered all of the wire part.

4 Finally add layers of the most sturdy and thickest petals at the bottom, where the petals might be damaged by the friction of the hand.

5 For the final decoration of the Tulipmelia make lines of wired Galanthus, Hypericum berries and pearls. Prepare them as closely to the wedding ceremony as possible for the sake of durability and carefully secure them with pearl headed pins. Finally attach one or two Fritillarias in the centre of the bouquet.

Design Inspired by the apple in the royal regalia I wanted to create something that rests naturally in the palm of the hand. It symbolizes both strength and fragility, reflected in the connection between the 'power' flower and the agility of the trailing part.
Technique Gluing technique with cold glue, to avoid damage to the fragile petals of the tulip. As mentioned above, use well watered tulips to get the desired and needed durability.
Emotions A piece of jewellery showing the fragility of life and the strength of marriage and togetherness! The ring on our finger signifies so much more in life that is so much more complex than we can fathom!

Colourful Flower Chain

Designer
Tomas

Materials
Beaucarnea recurvata / ponytail palm
Calamus rotang / rattan palm
Dianthus / carnation
Lunaria annua / annual honesty
natural spool wire
silver-coloured bullion wire

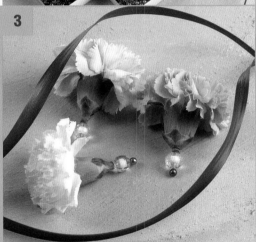

1 This bouquet requires a fairly small amount of material, which also has a very long shelf life. Select flexible but quite strong pulp cane to ensure the stability of the construction. Select the colour of the decorative pins based on the colour of the flowers.

2 Because of the size of this bouquet it is advisable to draw the design first on a scale of 1:1. Draw circles of different sizes, in a random pattern. Then start making the round shapes. Connect the ends of every branch with wire. Make sure the circles are not too large otherwise they will lose their playful character. Connect the circles according to the pattern you have drawn. Alternate large circles with small circles. Attach at least three circles to every circle to ensure the stability of the arrangement.

3 Prepare the flowers before putting them in the bouquet. The carnations are cut short. Put some cold glue on the decorative pins and insert them into the flowers. If necessary cut off a part of the pins, should they be too long.

4 Divide the flowers over the entire net of circles. Use cold glue once again to secure them to the circles. Mix colours for a better and stronger end result.

Design A 'special' design; the circles of pulp cane give the arrangement a playful and transparent character. This is a relatively simple bouquet with a maximum of 'body'.
Technique Preparing and making the circles takes up most of the time. Then the flowers are attached to the circles using cold glue.
Emotions Happiness is in small things, and lots of small moments make one big entity. Focusing on those moments will add colour to a marriage: moments of happiness, beauty and colour, just like the flowers in this bouquet.

69

Fruits of Love

Designer
Per

Materials
Fragaria / strawberry (fruit)
Jasminum / jasmine
Lathyrus odorata / sweet pea
Limonium 'Emille' / sea lavender
Phalaenopsis / moth orchid
all kinds of ribbons
bullion wire
floral foam sec
glue gun
pearl headed pins
pins
plastic ribbons
plastic water tubes
18-gauge wire

Design Playing with the concept of flowers and ribbons, working out dominance in ribbons to explain flowers and fruits with the help of colours and textures. The handbag shape with ribbons of all kinds emphasizes the playfulness of the whole idea. When carried, the focus will be on the flower part, the ribbons working as a backdrop for the flowers.
Technique Regular arranging technique in tubes and foam, in which the need of each individual material decides. Pinning and gluing are used for the structure of foam and ribbons. Always adjust the techniques and mechanics accordingly!
Emotions A warm summer day, full of flowers and fruits, skirts and curtains blowing in the wind, time spent on the countryside. That is also a way to translate and explain emotions for the uncomplicated summer bride.

1 The basis of this handbag design is created from floral foam which is cut in the desired shape, two bricks glued onto each other. Glue on plastic ribbons as a backdrop to all other vertical more or less free hanging ribbons.

2 Before fastening all ribbons, make the handle and fix it deep into the foam with U-shaped wires. The handle is made from 18-gauge wires taped together and covered with bullion wires of several colours. The ribbons are then pinned both on the inside and the outside of the shape.

3 Finalize the ribbon part with a layer that is hanging free on the outside and pinned only at the inside. Place plastic water tubes inside the lowered surface of the foam as a water supply for the more fragile flowers.

4 When placing flowers, vines and fruits, try to create a slightly domed profile. It will add lightness and elegance to the design and connects to the vertical hanging lines of the ribbons. Also add some longer vines of Jasmine trailing all the way down to the end of the ribbons to get a more flowery expression.

71

Tied

Designer
Max
Materials
Dendrobium / Dendrobium orchid
Dendrochilum cobbianum
Gypsophila paniculata / baby's breath
Hydrangea
Phalaenopsis / moth orchid
Clear Life spray
cold glue
wooden ball
nylon wire
silver-coloured spool wire
silver spray paint

1 Cut away the side twigs from the Gypsophila; these side twigs will be tied together to create a teardrop form, albeit a very compact one so that it will still look good when it has dried. Take a long piece of nylon wire and tie it to the first Gypsophila, then continue the tying process by wrapping the wire in spool wire. Make sure you work in a very regular way and stick to the shape.

2 Take a wooden ball with a diameter of 5 to 7 cm and spray paint it silver. Attach the ball to the nylon wire at about 8 cm above the Gypsophila. Secure the top of the teardrop form to the Gypsophila with glue to achieve a perfect shape. Treat the arrangement with Clear Life spray to improve the durability.

3 Select the hard Hydrangea flowers and cut them off the stalks. Secure them one by one in a very compact way with glue across the top of the teardrop form and thin them out at random as you work your way downwards.

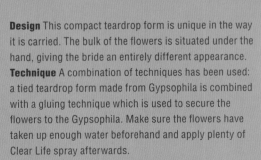

Design This compact teardrop form is unique in the way it is carried. The bulk of the flowers is situated under the hand, giving the bride an entirely different appearance.
Technique A combination of techniques has been used: a tied teardrop form made from Gypsophila is combined with a gluing technique which is used to secure the flowers to the Gypsophila. Make sure the flowers have taken up enough water beforehand and apply plenty of Clear Life spray afterwards.
Emotions The heavy-looking shape hanging from the nylon wire provides a certain amount of tension, but because of its agility the bouquet is still quite frivolous. This arrangement highlights the personalities of the bride and groom.

4 Apply the same procedure for the Dendrochilum and then for the flowers of the mini-Dendrobium. Work in layers to create optical depth. Finally work in the Phalaenopsis; do not use too many flowers, otherwise you will make the shape and structure disappear. Treat the arrangement once again with Clear Life spray.

73

Passion!

Designer
Tomas

Materials
Gloriosa rothschildiana / glory lily
Xerophyllum tenax / bear grass
red pearls on wire
red spool wire
red spray paint
wire (0,8 mm)

1 This bouquet is made using a minimum of flowers and decorative materials, and obviously requires the right choice in terms of shape, colour and flowers used.

2 Bend eight iron wires into a curve and attach them to a ring with a diameter of 4 cm. Spray paint this base red. Then weave a construction from the centre towards the outside just like a spider would do. Cover the ends with pearls to avoid the sharp edges damaging the wedding dress.

3 Next use pearl-headed floral foam wire to braid a construction that will be used as a base for the flowers. The more braiding you do, the stronger the base will become. Stick to the triangular shape in order to achieve the desired design. For a more elegant style and/or a taller bride you can also use the cascading waterfall style.

4 Weave the bear grass in-between the wire. The bear grass not only has a decorative value, but also a functional one: it offers a more solid base for the flowers.

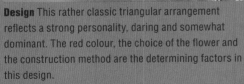

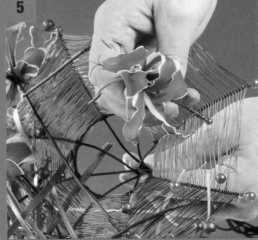

5 Finally, prepare the flowers by putting a decorative pin at the bottom of each little stem and wrapping the stem in decorative wire. Dip the top of the pin in cold glue before putting the pin into the stem. This secures the pin properly and also avoids loss of water, which improves the storage life of the bouquet. Next weave the flowers in-between the wires and the construction. Use cold glue in certain places to secure the flowers properly. Insert the flowers at different heights and depths to create an extra dimension. Finally drape some bear grass on top of the flowers.

Design This rather classic triangular arrangement reflects a strong personality, daring and somewhat dominant. The red colour, the choice of the flower and the construction method are the determining factors in this design.

Technique Shaping the spider web construction with decorative spool wire is the most time-consuming element. Afterwards a veil of pearls and wire is created as a base for the flowers. The flowers are braided and also secured with glue. Be aware of the Gloriosa's pollen: make sure you take out the stamen in order to avoid stains.

Emotions The language of flowers communicates through shape, colour and choice of flowers. The strong character, the passion and the daring colour of the Gloriosa are translated into the character of the bride.

75

A Green Start of ...

Designer
Max

Materials
Angelica archangelica / garden angelica
Aristolochia / Dutchman's pipes
Asclepia 'Moby Dick' / 'Moby Dick' silkweed
Chrysanthemum 'Yoko Ono'
Dendrochilum cobbianum / Dendrochilum orchid
Galax / beetleweed (leaves)
Hydrangea
Ligustrum / privet
Phalaenopsis / moth orchid
Wisteria / wisteria
grass
cotton wool
floral tape
ribbon
several floral wires

1 Remove the leaves from the Aristolochia, then plait the tendrils into a natural pattern to achieve a look of intertwined strands, varying in length from 20 to 60 cm. Allow the end of the arrangement to finish in a single tendril in order to maintain a natural appearance.

2 Cut the flowers and the other botanical materials at the desired length (see large photograph for a good estimate). Wrap the ends of the stems in wet cotton wool and secure them with floral wire (0,7 to 0,9 mm, depending on the weight of the material). Tie up the cotton wool and the stems with floral tape to avoid any loss of moisture and to give the arrangement a nice finishing touch.

3 Assemble the bouquet: the Aristolochia strands which have been put on wire are meant to trail down the hand; they are the base of the bouquet. Lines are created from this starting point and flowers can be worked in. Ensure the stability of the arrangement by properly tying it up.

4 Finish off the bottom neatly using Galax leaves. Finish off the stem as well with a green ribbon: secure the ribbon with little pins at the top of the stem, wrap the ribbon vertically round the stem and secure it once again at the top, then move down and up again in a spiral movement. Secure the ribbon with a pin and cut it.

Design Green is the main colour of this arrangement. The materials are processed in a rather traditional way; however the bouquet is also given a personal touch, amongst others because of the way the Aristolochia has been processed.
Technique This design uses the traditional wiring technique, which can be applied to a lot of bouquets. It is one of the basic techniques in flower arranging.
Emotions The colour green, which refers to a new beginning in nature, also refers to a new beginning here, i.e. marriage. The intertwined tendrils of the bouquet reflect the idea of how two lives are intertwining in marriage.

Silent Language of Love

Designer
Per

Materials
Fritillaria meleagris / fritillary
Hypericum / St. John's worth
Jasminum / jasmine
Salix / willow
cold glue
Mizuhiki wire
sewing pin / needle
spool wire

1 Prepare your materials before making the actual structure. Cut the Fritillarias at the right length, pin a Hypericum onto each stem and secure with cold glue. Make wires of 5 cm long cut Salix stems and pearl lines of Hypericum berries.

2 Make the structure by crossing the Mizuhiki wires in the middle; twist them around each other two to three times. Start with two wires and add new ones, continuously crossing and twisting them until you reach the desired shape.

3 Start at the top of the dome, working your way sideways and backwards before starting your descent. Keep in mind the profile of the work, allowing space for the hand, created by adjusting the distance between each wire.

4 As a handle create a twin ring fitting. Create each ring from double wires and attach the four ends to the structure. Then cover all ends with Salix and Hypericum as protection.

5 For the actual flower part start with lines of materials. Cross and entwine some of these, weave in the Fritillarias and Jasmins and finish by securing everything with some more lines. When well done no other fixing is needed. Also try to use size graduation when placing materials; apply the bigger materials at the top and gradually use smaller ones as you go downwards.

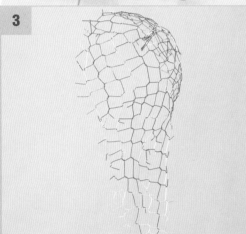

Design The intention is to create a lightweight, easy and comfortable to carry design. The twin ring fitting is a very useful and easy way to carry a wedding design. The wire structure also allows us to work transparently, showing the fragility and softness of the Fritillarias.
Technique Being exact and correct while making this 'hand made chicken wire' is of utter importance. If you have problems visualizing the structure, draw it life-size on a piece of paper and work on top of it. Remember to work irregularly within the structure.
Emotions A sensation of spring, caused by the fragility of the tender flowers, combined with the power and promise of summer. Just like that message in the first stirring feelings of love, dreaming of a lifetime together!

Summer Romance

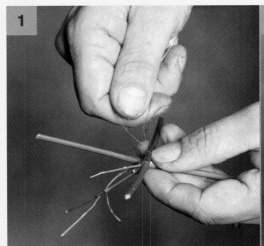
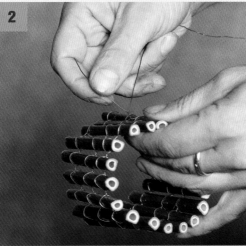

Designer
Max

Materials
Angelica archangelica / garden angelica
Bambusa / bamboo
Campus
grasses (various types)
Lonicera / honeysuckle
Nerine bowdenii / Guernsey lily
Rosa / rose (various types of rose buds)
cold glue
green spool wire

Design A trailing bouquet which is worn as a bracelet.
The structure of the bamboo is dominant but at the
same time it supports the shape and technique.
Moreover it is quite agile which gives this arrangement
a very interesting appearance.

Technique The connections which have been created
with wire are a very important aspect of this design;
make sure that all the connections are solid. To give the
arrangement some extra stability, you can spray it with
some spray glue. The flowers are secured with glue.
Treat the stems of the flowers with wax beforehand in
order to avoid loss of water.

Emotions The arrangement radiates a fertile late
summer feeling with its warm colours and typical
materials, relaxed yet displaying a cheeky shape
and personality.

1 Cut the bamboo (with a diameter of about 5 mm) into
pieces of about 8 cm and connect them with three green
spool wires. Make sure the wires are tightened
simultaneously so that they all run parallel to one another.
Connect the ends at the desired size (like a bracelet).

2 Strip the leaves off the bamboo and cut these into
pieces, varying in size from 2 to 11 cm. Roll the longest
pieces together starting from the middle of the twigs,
until you achieve a compact shape of about 40 cm long.
Make sure the bamboo points in all directions.

81

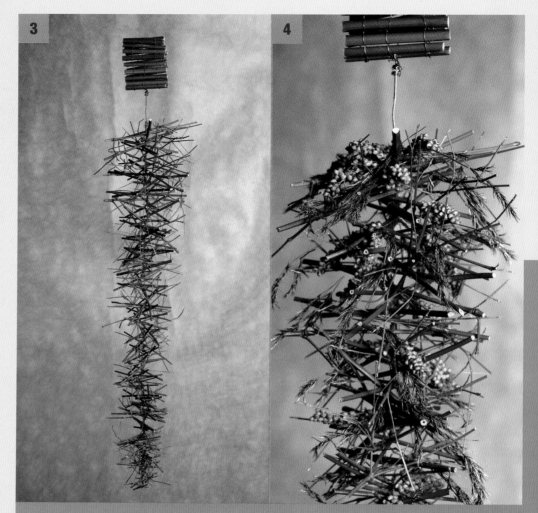

3 Attach the bracelet to the bamboo hanger, leaving a space in-between of about +/- 7 cm. Cut several types of grass into smaller pieces and secure these horizontally to the bamboo structure with glue, at the top somewhat closer together and thinning out as you go downwards. The bouquet should look nice from all sides, so make sure that you work with the same precision in all directions.

4 Next apply the same procedure to the other materials. First put in the various types of rose buds, then work in the more fragile flowers such as the Nerine. Create a full top with the Angelica and fill it in with the smaller flowers. Finally bring some lines into the bouquet using the Campus and the Lonicera.

Waterfall of Elegance

Designer
Tomas
Materials
Dischidia
Eucharis amazonica / Amazon lily
Ornithogalum arabicum / Arabian star flower
Spathiphyllum / Peace lily
cold glue
decorative ribbon
floral foam bouquet holder
rigid cardboard
wool (different thicknesses)

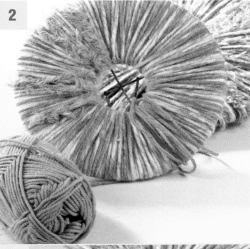

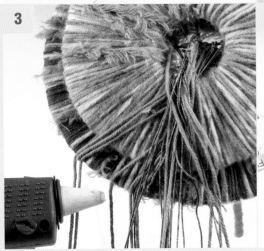

Design The two circles are the main ingredients of this design, the emphasis being on the simplicity of materials and colours used. The flowers spring up from the central point just like a waterfall, giving the design a stylish and elegant character.

Technique Wrapping the two circles in wool takes up most of the work. The wool is wrapped from the inside out until a complete circle has been formed. To give the structure more stability both circles are glued onto a bouquet holder. The woolen strands from which the flowers are hanging, are tied to the bouquet holder.

Emotions The two circles are the symbol of two partners forming a unity together whilst still maintaining their individuality. The green/white colour scheme is a deliberate choice, symbolising once again the aspect of duality. The soft wool provides an additional romantic finishing touch.

1 The design of this bouquet is based on green-white colours. In order to achieve a solid base, we use a bouquet holder. A ready-made sisal cylinder is used as a handle.

2 Cut two circles from a piece of rigid cardboard with a diameter of 15 and 18 cm respectively and make an opening of about 4 cm in both. Wrap the circles in wool of different colours and thicknesses. Make sure you always start from the optical centre. Secure the smallest circle to the bouquet holder with hot glue.

3 Slide the largest circle over the handle of the bouquet holder underneath the smaller circle so the bouquet holder sits in-between. Then tie strands of wool – in different lengths – to the core of the bouquet holder. Secure the wool with glue to the side of the largest circle to avoid it starting to move or forming one big spool.

4 Cover the base with flowers, putting the lilies on the ends. Wrap the Eucharis flowers in wool to give them extra stability. Attach the flowers on different heights, as this will create a dynamic effect. Finally glue the small Ornithogalum flowers onto the circles.

Reflection of Two Souls

Designer
Max
Materials
Bromelia
Dipladenia
orchids (various types)
Phalaenopsis / moth orchid
Rosa rugosa / Turkestan rose
tendrils
Clear Life spray
coloured plastic wire
copper tape
wax

Design This contemporary, expressive bouquet which is filled with details as far as the choice of flowers and materials is concerned, is special because of the unusual technique that has been used to create it. It is an extraordinary reflection for an extraordinary bridal couple.
Technique The special feature of this technique is the use of decorative tape to secure the material and to construct the arrangement. It is a nice example of the fact that we not only keep progressing in our professional domain, but we also keep searching for new solutions.
Emotions A reflection of two people facing life together, who are open to innovation, who greatly enjoy all the events that are taking place around them, full of confidence about the future.

1 Create a circular-shaped handle of thin red plastic wire which is also large enough to be used as a bracelet. Allow two long wires to come out from the bottom and connect these again with and through each other. Secure the wire with copper tape. The arrangement is meant to touch the floor and can even trail along the floor a little. Trim the flowers and dip the stems into wax. Make sure that the flowers have taken up plenty of water. Remove the leaves from the tendrils.

2 Start by putting the tendrils into the bouquet and fix them with copper tape. Allow the tendrils to fall through the bouquet just like the plastic wires, but with less dominant curves.

3 Put the waxed flowers into the bouquet and secure them with tape.

4 Work in the flowers using an airy and irregular pattern. Try to avoid creating parallel lines.

87

Straight through the Heart

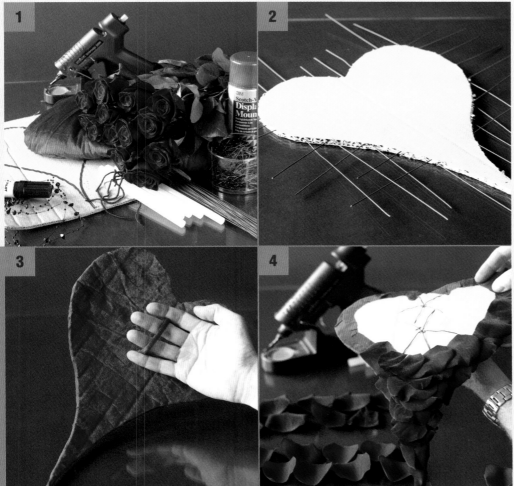

Designer
Per
Materials
Rosa 'Black Baccara' / 'Black Baccara' rose
bullion wire
cardboard
glue gun
pearl headed pins
pearls
spray glue
velvet
20-gauge wire

1 Collect all materials and put the roses in warm water so they are well watered when you use their petals. Draw a heart shape on a piece of double or triple layered cardboard.

2 Once you have cut out the heart, reinforce it by piercing 20-gauge wires into it, both horizontally and vertically. This will add stability and enables you to bend the heart into the desired profile.

3 Cover the backside of the cardboard with red velvet using spray glue. Also make a ring fitting/handle from 20-gauge wires; use five wires and tape them with floral tape. Pierce the handle through the cardboard and secure. Cover the back part with the same velvet.

4 Organize the rose petals according to size and colour before you start gluing them. Start at the edges using the biggest ones and work your way inwards with increasingly smaller petals.

Design A Rosemelia in the shape of a heart, a combination of the two strongest symbols of love. The red rose has always been the symbol of love, and the heart...well, Amor was good with his arrows!
Technique Gluing technique in which I personally prefer using a glue gun for the sake of speed, even though it might cause some burn damage on the petals. Since each petal is covered with another one, possible damage will not be visible. Moreover the durability of the Rosemelia is not affected.
Emotions Is there a better way to express love? This design speaks for itself!

Straight through the Heart

5 Bend the heart and create a softly curving profile before gluing the petals onto it. The curve will rest beautifully on the hand and will also give support.

6 Finally attach a beautiful whole rose head in the centre of the design – in this case I chose to put the centre a bit more to the right to attract attention. This does not only add focus but also creates a beautifully domed profile.

7 Add some decorative accents by using lines of irregular black pearls trailing down from the centre. This accentuates the blackness of the rose and adds movement to the Rosemelia.

Love is Never Ordinary

Designer
Per
Materials
Dianthus / carnation
Fritillaria imperialis / fritillary
Gloriosa rothschildiana / glory lily
Hypericum / St. John's worth
Limonium 'Emille' / Sea lavender
Phalaenopsis / moth orchid
bullion wire
chiffon ribbons
floral tape
Mizuhiki wire
pearl headed pins
plastic strings
20-gauge wire

1 Start by wiring and taping all carnations, while leaving open one cm at each flower head. Draw a perfect circle on a piece of paper and put all carnations on that line. Bend the stems 90 degrees at the binding point in the centre.

2 Secure the binding point with spool wire and connect each Carnation head with Mizuhiki wires. Use some additional wires to create a stabilizing crossed wire grid inside the circle. Also work in some Limonium and tie onto the binding place.

3 Cut all wires and stems at 10 to 12 cm underneath the binding point, tape them together and add long lengths of different ribbons for the trailing part cover. Secure this with horizontally circled ribbons and finally attach a pearl headed pin in a matching colour.

4 Prepare the flowers by either making a decorative end with bullion wire and pin or by replacing the stem by a Mizuhiki wire. Also make some lengths of Mizuhiki wires with Hypericum berries pierced onto them. See to it that all materials are fresh and watered.

5 To create the actual decoration inside the Carnation circle, use the back of the Carnation heads as a basis into which all materials are pierced and secured. Work in a crossed and overlapping manner and finish by securing everything with some Mizuhiki wires attached at both ends.

Design This design proves that carnations are not at all ordinary! They have great potential in all kinds of designs, even more so in wedding designs. Creating a geometric structure with their shape and colour, the carnations emphasize the small and fragile flowers in the centre of the bouquet!

Technique Old-fashioned but reliable wiring and taping technique as a base, with more wiring and piercing for the decorative central part. Always remember to use enough pressure when wiring and taping and to use well watered flowers.

Emotions Relaxed, almost casual in its expression. A design that fits many brides, all depending on the colours used. The one described here is suitable for a casual, modern, alternative girl, but think of white or dark red ... all different women!

Royal Grace

Designer
Tomas
Materials
Ceropegia woodii / string of hearts
Craspedia globosa / golden drumstick
Phalaenopsis / moth orchid
decorative wire (gold, purple, pink)
gold spray paint
pearls
sand
spray glue
wire (0,4 mm)
wire (0,7 mm)

1 First of all look for a few round shapes that you can model the wires on. Use two different wire thicknesses: 0,7 and 0,4 mm. Make about 40 curly shapes in different sizes.

2 Four circles are the base of this bouquet: two large ones which determine the size of the bouquet and two smaller ones which will constitute the inner diameter. Connect the top parts of the small and large circles. The space in-between the circles can now be filled with the curls. When putting these in, use a playful and not too static approach. Once both circles have been filled we connect the top parts once again and fill the bottom part with the remaining curls.

3 Spray the construction that has been created with gold paint and scatter a small amount of fine sand onto the wet paint to achieve a certain texture. Repeat this several times until you have achieved the desired effect. Then attach some pearls to gold-coloured decorative wire and secure them onto the circles. Allow the little pearls to 'float'.

4 Finally attach a few loose golden strands to the construction. Feed the wire through the nose of the Phalaenopsis and attach this to the arrangement. Make sure that you let the flowers float. This way a very special and airy design is created.

Design Quite often it is not easy to find a good balance between the base and the flowers. The strength of the golden object as opposed to the strength of the flowers gives this bouquet a very special look. Although both are noble in feeling and colour, they are each other's opposite as far as texture or material is concerned. The curly shapes combined with the orchids make this arrangement look almost royal.
Technique Turning the rigid metal wire into curly shapes and securing them in the shape of the bouquet is the most important aspect of this extraordinary arrangement. All the individual elements are put together like a puzzle until they become a harmonious entity. The flowers are floating around and through the little basket because we have hung them from strands.
Emotions The flowers are cherished by the little golden handbag. Luxury, safety and security represent the emotional part of this design. Yet, the flower makes a clear statement, without being robbed of any strength when facing the dominant construction.

Future, creations & step-by-step instructions
Per Benjamin (SE)
Max van de Sluis (NL)
Tomas De Bruyne (BE)

History
Per Benjamin (SE)

Drawings
Kathy van de Sluis-Kim (NL)

Photography
Kurt Dekeyzer (BE)
Helén Pe (SE)
Viktor and Natalia Smirnov (RU)
Pim van der Maden (NL)

Translation
Taal-Ad-Visie, Brugge (BE)

Final Editing
Heide-Mieke Scherpereel

Layout and print
Group Van Damme, Oostkamp (BE)

Published by
Stichting Kunstboek bvba
Legeweg 165
B-8020 Oostkamp
Belgium
tel. +32 50 46 19 10
fax +32 50 46 19 18
info@stichtingkunstboek.com
www.stichtingkunstboek.com

ISBN: 978-90-5856-309-5
D/2009/6407/3
NUR: 421

Per

Max

Tomas

life³

a bundle of creativity www.life3.net

Life3 is an international partnership consisting of
Per Benjamin, Max van de Sluis and Tomas De Bruyne.
Per started working with flowers at an early age,
almost by accident, and now has his own consulting
agency, Benjamins Botaniska in Stockholm. Tomas is a
floral designer who brightens up events and happen-
ings worldwide. He has a consulting agency in Belgium
and is an internationally established value.

They have all worked in various fields of the flower
industry, ranging from nurseries, wholesalers and retail
shops, and each of them is devoted to both commercial
and artistic designs focusing on the emotional side of
flowers. Per, Max and Tomas value the importance of
training and give demonstrations and classes all around
the world as well as in their home countries.

Per, Max and Tomas have taken part in many
competitions and have won several medals both
nationally and internationally. At the 2002 World Cup in
the Netherlands they were first, third and fifth
(respectively Per, Max and Tomas). In the aftermath
of the competition, they ended up talking and
commenting each other's works. Once they got talking,
they started playing with the idea of working together
in the future. It soon became clear that they shared the
same ideas and visions. Only half a year later, Life3
was born.

Life3 stands for emotions, creativity, craftsmanship
and communication. This partnership, the first of its
kind between three florists, aims to add new value to
the flower industry. It wants to take floral design up to
new levels and wishes to bring it to a wider audience.
Life3 offers demonstrations, workshops, decorations,
shows, seminars and books – both educational and
purely inspirational – and education for small and big
groups. They offer trend information, product design
and development, everything within the world of
flowers and beyond.